Praise for

STACKED AGAINST THE ODDS

"*Stacked Against the Odds* is a story of one family's triumph and victory as they navigate the challenging waters of raising a child with autism. Written in his own words, this inspiring account of Jesse Horn is encouraging and uplifting as Jesse walks us through his darkest times and greatest victories! Jesse and his family's true character are revealed for us as we take a ride with them through their story, giving us all hope and inspiration!"

–Don Teel
President, Speed Stacks, Inc.®

"If you're looking for inspiration on overcoming tough odds, look no further than Jesse Horn's first book *Stacked Against the Odds*. Jesse's story is an honest and heartwarming account of growing up with autism and the challenges it presents for a family. His accomplishments as a stacker are overshadowed only by the grit and determination he demonstrates in overcoming circumstances that would be overwhelming for most of us. If you need a bright spot to walk towards, read this book."

–Larry Goers
CEO, Speed Stacks, Inc.®

"*Stacked Against The Odds* is a valuable resource to any family who is experiencing the challenges faced by a child who is on the spectrum. Jesse takes a stand for those given an autism diagnosis and shares with us reasons why it isn't the end of the world, leaving the reader feeling hope and having faith in the possibility of brighter days ahead. This heartfelt story is filled with authentic moments that connect the reader to the feelings of joy, sorrow, pain, triumph, defeat, and renewal of spirit, that remind us how precious life is, and that life is now. We each have one special gift, our purpose. I am so happy that Jesse found and embraced his gift as a professional speaker to inspire our world forward. To help us to understand that within us is a 'key' to unlock our passion. That if we listen to the whisper of our heart and follow it, we can each be guided to our own unique gift, giving us the strength and courage to be authentically ourselves. Thank you Jesse for being you, being brave, and for sharing your story!"

-Jacqueline Bambenek
Wellness Coach

"This book was well-written and informative. As I was reading, I laughed a little and cried a lot! Jesse's story is as amazing as he is, and anyone who gets the opportunity to read this will get quite a bit of knowledge about autism. It is definitely an eye-opener! I work with persons with autism and cannot tell you how much I appreciate this book."

-Virginia Daloisio
Retired Educator

"Jesse Horn is an extremely intelligent, well spoken, insightful young man. Jesse not only tells his personal story but the story of thousands of individuals who live with autism. He honestly and openly shares the struggles and blessings that come with living with autism. Aunt Lola and Uncle Paul believed in Jesse not because he has autism but because they took the time to understand him. They are the true heroes in Jesse's life.

It is evident that Jesse wants the world to know what is in the hearts of all individuals living with autism:
"We must all be included and accepted…."
"We all need a purpose…."
"We all want to be loved and truly have much love to give back."
"I will never NOT have autism."
"My autism is a part of me, but it does not define me. I define autism."

–Lily Rider
CESA 4
Director of Itinerant Services/Kompas Care
AT/Autism Educational Consultant

STACKED
AGAINST THE ODDS

*Life with Autism and
How a Unique Sport
Changed My Life*

JESSE L. HORN

With Foreword by Bob & Jill Fox,
*Founders of **Speed Stacks, Inc**® and the
World Sport Stacking Association*

www.ten16press.com – Waukesha, WI

This book is dedicated to
all of my amazing family and friends
(especially Aunt Lola and Uncle Paul).
I could not have done this on my own,
and I thank you for being my wings!

TABLE OF CONTENTS

FOREWORD:

It would be simple to look at the shelves of sport stacking trophies and medals won by Jesse Horn and declare him a champion. To us, however, Jesse represents a champion defined by far more than shiny hardware. He is a winner in life. And he is a warrior who shows up to fight for kids facing adversity through autism. His voice is one of genuine hope for parents with children on the autism spectrum, and he is an inspiration to anyone who has overcome obstacles or has obstacles to overcome.

This is a story of Jesse's climb to the top of the podium, and he's not done yet. It starts with a young boy diagnosed with autism who wouldn't talk or even make eye contact, and it finishes with a poised young adult making national television appearances and giving motivational speeches reaching thousands. Spend just a minute with Jesse, and his warm smile and personality will have you rooting for him from the get-go. Read about the challenges of his upbringing and the unwavering love and support from those around him, particularly his Aunt Lola and Uncle Paul, and you will be filled with awe and admiration.

When it comes to our team of family and friends, Jesse is a first-round pick. For us to witness what he has accomplished with 12 plastic cups and the life-changing doors that have opened for him is incredibly gratifying. Jesse is a remarkable champion who truly stacks up with the best, and we will continue to cheer for him near and far. His journey will move and inform you, he will touch your heart, and we guarantee that after reading this book, you will want Jesse on your team too.

-Bob & Jill Fox
Founders, Speed Stacks, Inc.®
and the World Sport Stacking Association

A NOTE TO MY READERS

Dear Reader,

I wish you knew how thankful I am that you chose to read my story about growing up with autism. In my book, I share with you the happy times, the sad moments, and how I moved forward in my life.

I hope you find a bit of you or your child or your classmate in my story and that I can help you make it through the next day, week, month, and lifetime.

My cups were not always stacked in my favor, and autism was not the only hurdle I have had to face. By sharing the personal side of my life, I want to give hope to families with kids on the autism spectrum, but this story can also certainly give hope to those with many different abilities.

There are steps forward for all of us in life. Sometimes they are not big steps, but they are steps and blessings that will come with happy tears, I promise. Reaching out to you all through my book is my way of trying to make a difference. My hope is that it makes a difference in your life and the lives of your children.

-Jesse Horn

CHAPTER ONE:
@mrstackingdude409

*"Surround yourself with the dreamers, the doers, the believers,
and thinkers; but most of all, surround yourself with those who see
greatness within you even when you don't see it yourself."*
~Simone Biles

Dear Sport Stacking Family,

I wish you knew that without you all, I would not be where I am today. If I had not found my passion for sport stacking and all of you, I would have missed out on so much. Every single one of you will always be the most special people in my life!

You are all like family to me. You all see me as "Jesse" and my autism makes no difference to any of you! When I told all of you for the first time that I have autism, you all accepted me for who I am and made me be a big part of the sport stacking community. It feels so heartwarming to know that I went from hardly having any friends at all to hundreds and thousands of friends from all around the world and am able to have conversations with you all face-to-face.

Since 2010, I have learned so much from competing at sport stacking competitions, but the best thing ever was creating new memories from amazing times I have had while being part of a worldwide family. I didn't just find a sport; I found my life.

—Jesse

"Brace yourself for the ultimate showdown between these two athletes. The competition? Sport Stacking with Speed Stacks®!

My eyes were glued to the screen as I watched a young girl, Jamie, prepare to go head-to-head against a huge, muscled body-builder guy named Franz. They each were standing in front of a table that held 12 specially designed cups that you could manipulate into different towers. Of course, Franz and his arms so full of muscles that they couldn't lie flat on his sides couldn't make a stack no matter how hard he tried, and Jamie blew him out of the water.

Little did I know that seeing that commercial on Nickelodeon at my aunt and uncle's house would change my life forever.

Within a few weeks, I had somehow convinced Lola to get me my own set of cups. While I'm sure she thought they'd end up in the back of my closet, within a few days, I was practicing nonstop every chance I got. I watched the training video Speed Stacks® sent with every set of cups they sold, and I practiced at least three to four hours every day. I was hooked!

Between the repetitive nature of the sport and my drive for perfection, my brain was on fire as I stacked those cups. Just like with any other athlete, it seems you work harder at being the best if you are following your passion. This passion, stacking cups, became my reason for being in this world. Intense, I guess you could say, but for me, it was what made me feel that I belonged. It was proof that I really was good at something, good enough to people.

Up until that moment, I had never had anything to call

my own. I had been living in a bubble of sorts and had nothing that made me stand out (at least in a good way). In my earlier years, school was not always easy, and part of that might be because I was struggling to fit in and understand the world like most of my peers, but through blurry glasses.

Eventually, all my teachers learned how important this passion for sport stacking was for me. That spring, one of my teachers, Chris, was having a talent show to raise money for her junior agriculture class's annual field trip. I couldn't contain my excitement when she asked me to present my sport stacking talent during the show!

Since I was not quite ready to do the speaking part of the presentation, my aunt helped me out by being the one to explain the official stacks of sport stacking and then I dazzled the crowd with my performance. It went great, and everyone seemed to be amazed by this sport and how fast I was.

That first performance was just the beginning of my journey to becoming an advocate for kids on the autism spectrum and their caregivers. Today, my presentations can inspire and motivate even adults in the working world who are not on the spectrum and who just sometimes need direction.

My passion did not falter and only seemed to grow. After stacking for almost three years, I took the plunge and made a YouTube channel. I laugh now thinking about my channel name: MrStackingDude409. (I have since simplified to just "Jesse Horn.") Anyway, I began making videos of my sport stacking that I shared with my YouTube friends.

The first time I ever said aloud to anyone that I had autism, it was on a YouTube video that I made. As a child, I asked my mom over and over what was wrong with me. "I hate being so different!" I'd yell. After months of this, she broke down and told me that I had autism, and she tried to explain what it meant.

She also said, "You absolutely cannot tell this to anyone at school. They'll only make fun of you. And they don't need to know."

I held it in for so long, but as I grew up, I realized that it was an important thing for me to say. It was important to who I am. It's important for people to understand what autism is and why I'm not ashamed that I have it. And so, when I was thirteen, I made a video and said, "My name is Jesse, and I have autism."

And I haven't looked back.

As I continued stacking, I learned that it was a real competitive sport and that there were tournaments around the country and the world. It was then my dream to compete in these tournaments and at the World Sport Stacking Championships and to meet all of my sport stacking friends in person. I knew I was fast enough to compete because I had been getting scores that put me in the top ten overall fastest sport stackers unofficially online. I had talked to my uncle about attending the World Sport Stacking Championships in 2009, but my uncle and aunt were just not sure I was ready to handle things like the noise, following the directions of the judges, and fear of me having a meltdown.

I kept doing what I could to convince them I was ready and told them about a tournament in Eagan, Minnesota. Luckily, that was not far from our home, and my uncle agreed that I could register. That was on March 6th, 2010, and it was the beginning of my chance to be with and compete against kids my age and finally feeling I fit in somewhere with my peers.

Before the tournament, Luke, one of my idols in sport stacking, messaged me. Luke lived in Eden Prairie which is near Minneapolis and Eagan. Luke was one of the fastest sport stackers in the entire world. He set world records and was featured on TV in an Incredible Edible Egg commercial. I tried hard to stack as fast as he could, and I knew that if I continued to practice, I might one day be as fast as he was. Anyway, Luke knew I was from Wisconsin and was signed up to compete at the Eagan tournament.

He asked me if I would like to come to his house the night before the tournament for a pizza party. I was so excited that my heart was pounding out of my chest. My mom agreed to let me attend as long as Lola and Paul were with me. Of course, that was no problem as the sport stacking world was all about families and building good kids, good sportsmanship, and a sport everyone could play. It left no one out! In fact, the youngest stackers competing were around four, the oldest in their sixties, and any disability was welcome. I was thirteen, and this was the first peer party I had ever been invited to and was able to attend. It was and will always be the best party I have ever attended.

This was a momentous occasion for me and for my family. Suddenly, the wall around me that kept me apart from everyone else began to crumble. I didn't need it like I once did. Oh, don't get me wrong, there are days when the door needs to open a bit to see just what your child on the spectrum can handle, and you may always carry that "what-if" fear." That, according to my aunt and uncle, doesn't ever completely go away. But really, does it ever go away even with your child without a disability?

I guess, to be honest, I also worry because I am not really totally worldly and there are many things I continue to need help with, and I may always need help with, so I do worry about the day that I may no longer have my aunt and uncle in my life. That does scare me a bit. But this first step into the real world changed my life forever!

The next day, we went to Eagan where the tournament was being held. My uncle said he was holding his breath, waiting to see if this would be just as great for me.

Now, the noise was always hard for me, and like many with autism, we normally need to cover our ears as noise is so much more intense for us than most. Also, people directing you to come to the competition table, saying when to start and stop, and telling you if you did the stack right or if it was a scratch was a bit scary. It sounds like a lot for someone with autism, but I walked in, handed my coat to my uncle, and said, "See you later!" and that's all she wrote! After I experienced the atmosphere and got through the prelims of the event, I was ready for the finals.

I was up against Luke in the 3-6-3 stack finals, and Luke was first to stack. He got 2.41 seconds in his 3-6-3 stack, and then it was my turn. I got 2.34 seconds in my 3-6-3 stack. I beat one of the best in the world in the 3-6-3 stack in my first ever sport stacking tournament. Everyone was so excited for me. Even Luke was happy for me. This is why the sport is one that lifts each stacker up to be the best and encourages us all to keep working at beating the last record we made.

Lifting the bar was exactly what I intended to do, and with the help of my aunt and uncle with some of the logistics, in April 2010, I took another big step and registered for the World Sport Stacking Championships in Denver, Colorado, home of the World Sport Stacking Association and Speed Stacks®. I was so excited, and it was also my first plane ride.

My uncle had promised me we'd take a plane ride. We were in the backyard, relaxing and watching a plane leave a jet trail in the big, bright, beautiful sky. It was as if God was writing a message just for me. I turned to Uncle Paul and said, "Uncle? I wish someday I can fly on a plane."

He looked me right in the eyes and said, "You know what, Jesse? Uncle promises you'll fly in a plane someday." As of today, thanks to my family, God, and the sport of sport stacking, I've been on over fifteen plane rides.

I was now definitely in training mode and practiced three to four hours a day. That year, the event was sponsored by Wonderful Pistachios, and I was on a relay team called "The Pistackios." One of the team's moms had ordered light green t-shirts with our team name printed on them.

In Denver, I also competed in a doubles event with one of my YouTube friends, Josh, who had been following my page and thought we would fit well together. It was the first time we had ever stacked together, but we rocked the house because of our score. We also made the "Stack of Champions" where each was given three more tries to actually better our score, and it brought us in third overall and we went home with trophies! Incredibly, that part was done on a big stage under lights with hundreds of people from all over the world watching. I don't think I have ever been happier!

Almost all of the competitors stayed at the Embassy Suites in Denver, and the hotel was fully in support of making our experience one we would never forget. It will always be my favorite world championships because whatever room door opened as you walked by, you would hear the sound of cups stacking. When you looked down from the balconies to the center court of the hotel, every table and every side room was full of kids stacking those cups and parents sitting around it all.

Paul and Lola could and still can nap while I am stacking cups about ten feet away. Everyone becomes accustomed to the sound. It's sort of like living next to a railroad track. You just don't hear it after a while.

Leaving the tournament, I felt extra aware of how lucky I was to be with other people doing what I loved. I knew I would be a bit lonesome because back home, there wasn't anybody I had close by who was sport stacking. So, I was again in my own little world and dreaming of the next tournament. Shortly after the World Sport Stacking Championships, I felt more comfortable with who I was and much more confident. I felt it was time to let my classmates and sport stacking community know that I had autism. It really made no difference to my sport stacking family that I had autism, but it still was a social stumbling block in school.

To some who do not understand the difference in how someone with autism looks at life, it can be very different and not like the so-called "norm." The view of life for those on the spectrum is nowhere near that. The comment was once made to me in that, "Sport stacking was sure going to take me places!"

Well, I kept attending tournaments. After traveling across the globe, from Denver to Montreal to places like the Bahamas, we can definitely say I've been in more places than most.

I got a phone call from Pola, the head coach of the U.S. national sport stacking team, in February of 2011. First of all, I never got phone calls because when you have autism, people do not call. Ever. I had a pretty good idea of why she was calling, and I knew exactly what I would say when she asked.

Pola said, "Hi, Jesse! I'm with Team USA, and I am calling to ask you if you would be interested in being on the team?"

How do you even react when your biggest dream has just been laid out there in front of you?

I stammered, "Y-y-yes!"

Pola said, "I thought you might say that, Jesse! Welcome to the team, and I look forward to seeing you at the world championships in Garland, Texas, in April. We'll be in touch." Well, it was time to step it up even more, so the intense practicing began. I had worked hard to reach this goal, and I was going to do my best in Garland for the coach and my team. I had finally found a place I fit in where I was just "Jesse" and not "Jesse, the kid with autism." I was practicing every spare minute of every day, videoing myself and showing my YouTube fans my progress.

In April 2011, we rented a car, and my uncle, aunt, and I began the long drive to Garland, Texas, for the World Sport Stacking Championships. The championships were held at the Special Events Center, a large complex in Garland that would be the home of not only the World Sport Stacking

Championships but also the Super Stack 2011. It was an amazing tournament, and I came home with two trophies.

The saddest thing for me, and I know for some of my teammates, is when we have to say goodbye and not see each other for probably another year. It is an empty feeling, especially for me who really did not fit in or have friends back home with the same interest or passion for sport stacking.

In our small world in Wisconsin, to be popular, you needed to be able to pass a football, make a basket, tackle, and pin, or hit a home run, and it wasn't hanging with the kid that stacked cups, which to most was a bit unusual. So needless to say, I was not going to get asked to hang with the local football players, but my autism made no difference to my sport stacking family, and I was very happy to have found my place in the world.

Summer vacation arrived, and I was finally free to keep growing and learning from the experiences of traveling to sport stacking tournaments in Illinois, Iowa, Missouri, and even the first annual Amateur Athletic Union (AAU) Junior Olympic Games Sport Stacking Championships that were held in Houston, Texas.

At this point, I was winning first overall stacker at almost every tournament I entered. When the World Sport Stacking Association announced that sport stacking had been invited to be one of the sports added to the AAU Junior Olympic Games, I was thrilled!

To compete, you had to officially qualify to participate by placing in the top ten for your age division at any sanctioned tournament that year in the United States or Canada. Luckily, I did and received my official invitation letter that said, "Congratulations, you have qualified for the 2012 AAU Junior Olympic Games!" Getting that letter for me was like winning the lottery. I was over the moon excited! I wanted to go so badly, but I did not come from a family whose budget could fully fund a trip that required airfare, hotel, and other expenses for me, my uncle, and aunt.

My aunt announced the good news on her Facebook page, and a friend, Lizzy, who was my mom's best friend and a friend of the family for years, noticed it and asked what she could do to help get me to the games. She suggested a bake sale, and my aunt thought that was a great idea. My mom was to have back surgery that summer, the day before the bake sale, so her friends Mary Lou, Patty, Liz, Trista (my sister-in-law), Lugene (my aunt's best friend), and many others started planning.

The support for contributing baked goods was overwhelming, and that was the first time I realized that my community was truly my extended family. Lizzy helped set up a bank account they called "The Jesse Horn Benefit" for donations, and my sister-in-law, Trista, who is in marketing, helped with making flyers and signs for the bake sale. Jars with the benefit name were put at local businesses, all in an effort to raise money in our small community to get me to Houston.

On June 30th, 2012, the big bake sale day was set up at our small community room located in our local fire station. There were cakes, cookies, brownies, pies, bars, a jar of the famous Branger family pickles, lap quilts, and more. It was a room full of deliciousness, and I was there demonstrating my stacking, and people were being so generous in donations and buying up all the goodies. I remember it was a very hot day and my aunt had borrowed a clown outfit from her friend, Jan, and stood outside by the road with a sign that said, "Bake sale this way!"

I am here to tell you it was amazing, and at the end of the day, we had raised enough money to fly to Houston for my first AAU Junior Olympic Games Sport Stacking Championships! I was at a loss for words and so grateful to residents of Buffalo City, Cochrane, Alma, Nelson, Fountain City, and the surrounding area for the support they gave me. Many of these people became supporters and were the reason I was able to get to tournaments. But what they really may not know is that taking me on as family played a major part in where I am today. I can never repay them all, but I do try and pay it forward whenever I can.

To thank everyone on a larger scale, my uncle and aunt got me set up to be in our community's annual Fourth of July parade that year. My uncle decorated their little red Kia Soul with flags and magnetic signs on the doors saying, "Thank you for the support!" and a big sign on the back window saying, "Texas Bound!" I stood up through the moon roof and threw out candy to all the little kids.

The next big step then was traveling by plane, which I love, to Houston, Texas. We arrived at the team hotel, and I had a day of practicing and hanging out with my sport stacking friends from all over the country.

After all the practice, I knew I was ready for the tournament and my competition. The first day is the day they call prelims, and if you place in the top ten in your age division, you can then move on to the finals the next day. I qualified for finals in all the individual stacks as well as the relay event. The big day was ahead, and I would be competing with the top ten in my age division. It was fun and a huge success! My individual times put me in the top fifteen overall out of over two hundred and fifty stackers. I proudly carried home one gold, four silver, and two bronze medals.

Also, I brought home a medal for being fourth overall in the relay event with my team and a trophy for being eighth overall in the 3-3-3 individual stack. What a great experience, and it would not have been possible if it wasn't for that community bake sale.

2013 and 2014 continued to be exciting years for me. In 2014, I was preparing for the annual AAU Junior Olympic Games Sport Stacking Championships that were being held in Des Moines, Iowa. My aunt and uncle always pumped me up with positive feedback to get me ready. They said to me, "Jesse, this Junior Olympics is going to be your best ever!"

I was a bit skeptical of their enthusiasm because it was a little over the top. We traveled to Iowa and stayed in the team hotel, which was so great as I got to just hang out with my sport stacking friends. The first day always includes an opening ceremony, and we all got settled in as Bob Fox and his son Kit were about to announce the winner of a very prestigious award: The Joel Ferrell Outstanding Performance Memorial Award. This award recognizes athletic ability and good sportsmanship to an athlete in each of the eighteen sports featured in the 2014 Junior Olympics.

Out of approximately 12,030 athletes competing in all eighteen events, twenty-seven athletes would receive this honor that year. Bob and Kit began sharing something about the 2014 winner, and all of a sudden, I realized they were talking about me. I, Jesse Horn, was going to be the 2014 Joel Ferrell Outstanding Performance Memorial Award winner. I was so humbled, excited, and shocked. My aunt and uncle did not share with me that they knew about this, but when they told me this Junior Olympics was going to be the best ever, they were so right! Hundreds of parents and stackers all stood up and gave me a standing ovation. For a kid on the autism spectrum who really never quite fit in, being honored by so many was beyond my dreams.

That year, I managed to be in the top fifteen overall fastest sport stackers at the 2014 Junior Olympic Games Sport Stacking Championships. Finishing out my 2014 sport stacking tournament season, I competed at tournaments in Michigan, Illinois, and at the 2014 U.S. National Sport Stacking Championships in Kansas City, Missouri. I had a fantastic year, and at the nationals, I finished as the fastest 17-18-year-old male and the ninth-fastest overall stacker out of over 250 competitors.

In the fall of 2014, Bob and Jill Fox invited me and Sarah, another stacker on the spectrum, to travel to St. Pete Beach, Florida, to the National Autism Conference. I had met Sarah before at a tournament, and she and her mom, Shelley, are very nice. Speed Stacks® was a vendor at the conference, and Sarah and I along with Bob and Jill would be working the Speed Stacks® booth. When we got there, we learned that Temple Grandin was going to be the keynote speaker. We were very excited to meet her because we all had heard of all she has accomplished through the years, even though she was diagnosed with autism at a young age.

We were in St. Pete for three days presenting sport stacking to those on the spectrum as well as those who worked with people on the spectrum. It was an amazing experience for both Sarah and me. Meeting Temple Grandin and sharing the tool of sport stacking was a wonderful way for Sarah and me to offer a possible tool for others on the spectrum to use that could possibly open up their world as it did for us.

My passion has kept me attending tournaments, and I decided that I would not attend the prom that year in order to attend a sport stacking tournament in Kansas City, Missouri. I still attended a couple of dances on my own and had some late nights finishing schoolwork to keep my grades up. We had a senior trip that took us all bowling and for a picnic at Lake Park in Winona, Minnesota. There were steaks on the grill and a bunch of silliness playing in the park that was truly needed by us all after all the years we put in to get to the big day.

The 2015 AAU Junior Olympic Games Sport Stacking Championships were to be held in Virginia Beach, Virginia, and I was practicing every day for at least an hour or two. Virginia Beach was beautiful. The beach was breathtaking day and night, and as you walked along the beach, you couldn't miss the enormous King Neptune statue that dwarfed even me at six foot two. I will always remember having the best-frozen custard that I have ever had.

The tournament as always was exciting, and I did pretty well. My individual scores put me third overall in the 17-18-year-old male division, and I took fourth overall in doubles with my good friend, Dominic. Even though I did not do as well as I expected of myself, I now know and finally, understand that it's so much more than the trophies. It truly is the memories you make that are the real prize.

CHAPTER TWO:
Warning Signs

*"Why fit in when you
were born to stand out?"*
~Dr. Seuss

Dear Doctor who diagnosed me,

I wish you knew how thankful I am that you were able to diagnose my autism when I was three years old. My family had been trying to figure out why I was not meeting the typical milestones other kids my age had and why I was so different from everyone else.

Without you, and not having that early diagnosis, I would never have had the ABA Therapy that is so important. My family finding out what they and I were dealing with was sad, but also a relief. Things could have turned out so much differently had I gone through life not knowing why I was so different and not having the opportunity to have the early intervention. Again, thank you so much from the bottom of my heart for discovering my diagnosis of autism. My hope is that someday I will be able to thank you in person.

-Jesse

I can pretty much guarantee that no one who knew me when I was about eighteen months would ever have thought that I would be a college graduate, let alone a world champion sport stacker, award-winning public speaker, and the author of a book.

It was around eighteen months old when my mom noticed the first real signs of concern. At first, she thought it was a fluke or a random occurrence, but more and more often, I began living in my own little world. It was like a light switch in my brain turned off between the ages of one and two. I was no longer making eye contact, I did not talk, and when my name was called, I made no sign of hearing the request.

This was the beginning of several months where my family was not at all sure of what was happening in my little world. They did what families do best, they gathered me up and put me inside a bubble to keep me safe. As time went on, though, they began to be fearful that I would never be able to accomplish things on my own outside that bubble.

I was terrified of loud noises like a vacuum cleaner, I did not understand cold from hot, and if I was told no, the world had come to an end for me and it could take an hour to calm me down and redirect me to something else. *Barney, Sesame Street, Bear in the Big Blue House*, and many other children's television shows were a big help in diffusing and redirecting my day. My family was always on edge and had to plan every minute of the day to help me get through it without being totally exhausted from the meltdowns.

On the other hand, some of the milestones that were

happening still seemed somewhat typical. I started crawling, backward, mind you, at eight and a half months but found front gear at nine months. I started to pull myself up on furniture at ten months and walked a little after twelve.

Just past the age of two, I was trying to say a few words, but all I was able to do was emulate what I was seeing on television. For example, I would count to ten with the *Sesame Street* characters, and I could say, Elmo and Barney. But other than that, my speaking was nonexistent. My mom longed to hear me say 'Mama' or 'Dada,' but sadly that did not occur until I was around four years old when I did say 'Mama'. It took another six months for me to say 'Dada' and 'Shaun,' who is my brother.

Playtime with family could be challenging. When I was about two years old, I was not understanding even relatively simple games like stacking cups to create a tower. I would push them over after my uncle had stacked them and immediately have a meltdown. So, my uncle would stack them up again to make me happy, but the outcome was the same. I am still not sure why or what was making that so hard for me. Lola and Paul always thought they could diffuse the meltdowns until one night when I was in the refrigerator trying to get the eggs out.

My aunt said she had to stand in front of the refrigerator to stop me, which caused a major meltdown. She picked me up and put me in my crib to try to redirect me, but I was just not calming down. During these meltdowns, I would scream, kick, cry, and literally NOTHING could redirect me. Not words, not treats, not anything. As hard as it was for my family to watch, they also knew how painful it must be for me, both physically and mentally.

My aunt called my mom and dad and told them about the meltdown, and they came to help. By the time they got there, I had calmed down and was sitting on my aunt's lap playing with a toy, but Mom thought it was best to take me home for the night.

Aunt Lola told me that night they held each other and cried, so scared of what may be happening to me and what the future for me would hold. A few months later, my mom and aunt talked about what they were seeing happening, and my mom began researching some of those things and was becoming very concerned that this was more than just a phase, and they decided it was time to seek a professional opinion.

Others in the family thought that they were probably overreacting and that they should just give it some time, urging them to wait. After all, they said, kids will do things on their own time.

When I was three years old, I was evaluated by the special education teachers at my school, and the summary from that evaluation basically confirmed my family's concerns about the delays they were seeing.

I would play with other children in the classroom but was really disinterested in them for the majority of the time. They saw delays in socialization; expressive, receptive, self-help, and fine motor skills; and language comprehension. I did things repetitively, and my language was limited, and thus my frustration levels were high. Their recommendations were for further testing. They felt that without intervention, my gains in any of these areas would be small.

In November of 2000, the Gilliam Autism Rating Scale showed that there was a likelihood of autism. The psychologist who oversaw that report ordered a complete assessment, including psychological, developmental, speech and language, audiological, and neurological elements. Depending on all those results, he felt there may be value in clarifying my appropriateness for more intensive services in both the area of speech and language and social interactional areas.

Well, this is pretty overwhelming, even for me to be sharing the inside work to get to what we all wanted: early intervention.

At age three years and eleven months, a speech/language evaluation was done with the conclusion that my auditory comprehension was age equivalent to a twelve-month-old child. My expressive communication was at an eleventh-month-old age equivalent, and my communication skills were significantly reduced for my chronological age. Communication and social behaviors observed supported a diagnosis of a speech/language disorder versus a speech/language delay. Intense, direct, and consistent speech/language therapy was strongly recommended. More therapy was suggested in addition to the speech therapy already being done through the school.

The audiological evaluation showed no sign of hearing loss, so luckily I was not faced with another hurdle there. The evaluation done by the psychologist concluded the diagnostic impression was that of autism. He also spoke to my mom about the Wisconsin Early Autism Project (WEAP), which offered early intervention services and was available in our area. My mom told him that she was very interested, and he offered to help her contact them once the medical doctor gave a final diagnosis.

We are almost there, but the medical evaluation now needed to be done by the doctor who could confirm the diagnosis and give a name to all the testing that had been done. I was almost four at this time, and the clock was ticking.

It is very important to get intervention as early as possible. So, if we could arrive at a diagnosis, we could then move forward.

Finally! There it was on the paper, that word I mentioned earlier. Diagnosis. My diagnosis was that I had an Autism Spectrum Disorder (ASD). The medical doctor also agreed with the psychologist that I would benefit from a variety of behavioral training through the Wisconsin Early Autism Project and that intensive speech and language therapy would be the most important approach towards my progress.

I don't remember much from when I was three, but I am sure it was a very stressful time for my family.

If you are reading this because someone in your family has been or could be diagnosed with autism, I want you to remember this word: HOPE. I'm sure you're terrified and exhausted and stressed, but you will be okay. It will all be okay, just hold on to hope. Besides, your child too could be a world champion of something someday!

CHAPTER THREE:
Reach Me

*"The price of success is hard work,
dedication to the job at hand, and the determination
that whether we win or lose, we have applied
the best of ourselves to the task at hand."*
~Vince Lombardi

Dear State Legislatures, U.S Congressmen,
U.S Senators, and Our President,

When I was diagnosed in 2001, autism had truly started to explode and has continued to increase, not decrease. I realize it is a condition that has a full spectrum of different levels, but I want you to know that those kids diagnosed with autism are the future of our country and the world.

So, I am asking that you continue to support the Autism CARES Act and fund research and the therapy needs of now one in fifty-nine kids being diagnosed on the autism spectrum. My therapists truly helped me to get where I am today.

I may not be realistic, but my family has always taught me to look for the positive, that with your continued support, you will give those of us diagnosed every chance to be accepted and included in this world.

–Jesse

Autism. I had it. Now what?

We lived in a small trailer, my mom didn't work, and now we needed to pay for all different kinds of therapy, behavioral interventions, and equipment. Of course, we all knew early intervention was essential, but it's a whole lot easier to say than to actually do it.

Thanks to a recommendation, my mom and dad turned to our county health and human services department to see if they could offer us any assistance to secure the Wisconsin Early Autism Project services.

That would take more work, a bit of stress, and sleepless nights completing the Katie Beckett application process. Katie Beckett is (or was at the time, at least) a special eligibility process that allows certain children with long-term disabilities, mental illness, or complex medical needs, living at home with their families, to obtain a Wisconsin ForwardHealth Medicaid card. The card could cover not only medical costs at the doctor but also the ability to secure the services offered by the Wisconsin Early Autism Project.

I qualified for Katie Beckett and as well qualified for a few other programs that would help me get the early intervention that was so needed. The Lovaas method of applied behavioral analysis is a world-renowned leader in early comprehensive behavioral treatment for young children with autism. Research has shown that with early comprehensive treatment based upon the principles of applied behavioral analysis, children with autism can make significant life-changing gains, and I am surely a poster child for that, and I am grateful to the state of Wisconsin and Governor Doyle. They helped make great strides in being proactive instead of reactive to the needs of kids being diagnosed on the autism spectrum.

The prevalence of autism in U.S. children according to the Center for Disease Control and Prevention (CDC) increased from one in one hundred and fifty in 2000 to one in sixty-eight in 2010, and today, the CDC has updated that number to one in fifty-nine children. Sadly, we still are no closer to knowing why.

Once I qualified for Katie Beckett, at age four, I needed to be evaluated again in Madison, Wisconsin, at the Early Autism Project office. The recommendations from their psychologists were that I should participate in Lovaas therapy, consisting of as many hours as possible (e.g. thirty to thirty-five hours) of one-on-one behavioral intervention each week at my home. The treatment was to address deficits that were noted in my verbal, nonverbal, language development and adaptive ability. The intervention was to be approached in a systematic and cumulative manner with clearly outlined objectives and methods by which my progress could be measured.

My caregivers were to continue a rich home environment that provided an opportunity to generalize my experiences into the real world. My family was an integral part of my treatment, and it was imperative that they remained involved with therapy and decisions regarding its course. The treatment was to focus on procuring skills of attending to visual and verbal cues, progressing to teaching more advanced receptive and expressive language skills. The intervention focused on social skills, particularly in communication and adaptive functioning, and then progressively building on skills that I had already mastered. Once I mastered all of that, the learning could then be generalized to interactive situations such as school and community. (I am sure glad I was pretty much oblivious to all of this, or I would still be in a meltdown mode. HA!)

Now that I had qualified to receive applied behavior analysis, the search for therapists who were trained or could be trained began. My mom agreed to thirty-two hours of therapy weekly. I do not remember how the scheduling of that was done, but I do remember the first names of several of my therapists: Heidi, Jen, Matt, Beth, and more. Therapy was set up and done in the bedroom of my home. There was a table in the corner where the therapist and I would play, learn how to make eye contact, and talk. I remember them rolling me up in my favorite blankets with balloons on them.

I think that was a way of teaching socialization, but it was also a way of calming me down. Maybe the pressure of blankets around me was what helped. I do know others on the spectrum are comforted by weighted blankets, which are blankets that have specially formulated weights in them to provide security. My mom purchased reinforcers for the therapists to use.

Applied Behavioral Analysis (ABA) works on repetitive acts that work towards the child being able to find the correct answer or action. The child is given a reinforcer that encourages the outcome to be consistent (e.g. a child learns a word like *car*). A reinforcer for me was being rolled up in my blankets, high fives, or a small toy or food that would give me a signal that I had done well and deserved recognition for the accomplishment.

Now, remember, I was over four years old and attempting to learn things that are normally achieved at age one or two. It took the therapists much patience and dedication, and they all wanted me to make progress each day. Sadly, some days I was just not having it, and not getting a reinforcer was when the meltdowns would flare.

One of my best, treasured memories was when the therapists were working on socialization. One of my therapists, Heidi, and my mom planned a pool party day. Heidi brought her two sons, Joseph and Ben, over to swim in the little plastic pool my mom set up on our front deck. I have a picture of that day, and I was all smiles and had so much fun. I don't think I really looked at them, but all three of us splashed around and had snacks after. Having a friend even then felt really great! In those early years, this was something that I had little experience with. Yes, that is a bit sad, but so many on the spectrum face this in one way or another.

As the pieces of therapy were put in place, my family also learned from it and did what they could to build on the goals my therapists were striving to reach for me.

I was there, ready to be reached.

CHAPTER FOUR:
One Word at a Time

"I am different. Not less."
~Dr. Temple Grandin

Dear Teachers,

I wish you knew how much I appreciate all the help, love, and support you have given me throughout the years! I want to express how special I felt being one of your students during my grade school-college years! Every single one of you saw me as "Jesse" and not just that student with autism. I feel so lucky to have had a group of teachers like you.

You all made my grade school-college experience so special. I will always remember each and every one of you. Not only were you all dedicated to teaching your students, but you also took the time to understand the obstacles that kids face, such as autism.

Whenever I had a problem or just had a bad day, you all were always there to calm me down, make me feel better, and feel loved. Without you all, I would not have made it this far in life. You all were always there and had the patience to help me with whatever I needed help with.

You all make a big difference in each of the students' lives, and it was always obvious how much you all truly cared about the happiness and success of your students, like me. Again, thank you so much from the bottom of my heart for being my teachers and being there whenever I needed you. You will always be some of the most important people in my life!

-Jesse

Each weekday morning, a van would pull up in front of our house. Jan and Lori, the drivers, were a huge part of my early years, and while I don't have super clear memories of those days, I definitely remember them. It was almost impossible for me to ride a school bus. When you took my inability to communicate and mixed it with all the noise and movement, it was a pretty much-guaranteed meltdown in the making.

My aunt told me that each morning my mom would carry me out and put me in the car seat and get me buckled in. This helped with the transition because, at that age, I did not tolerate being picked up by others. My teacher in preschool was Jill, and I had an aide, Jenny, who had also been one of my Wisconsin Early Autism Project therapists who helped direct me through my day. I remember the circle rug and circle time, where some days the teacher would read or teach us about the calendar. When there were updates on my progress, the teacher shared that I liked circle time, but I would always sit on the outside of the circle close to the other kids, but still far enough away to avoid direct eye contact with them or the teacher.

My home routine, as well as the new steps in attending school, was always kept the same. Repetition was important, and using visual learning tools such as videos helped me learn and feel comfortable as I faced each new challenge.

I spent most weekends at my aunt and uncle's house down

the street. What started as respite care had turned into our routine. Slowly, weekends here and there had just turned into every weekend. My mom trusted Lola and Paul the most, and Lola told me that after a while, they couldn't live without me!

Their home was comfortable and relaxing for me. They had most of the videos I liked, and, of course, the puppet theater that Aunt Lola bought. Uncle Paul would always make the puppets come alive with his stories and voices for each puppet.

The little theater was a blue curtain, hung by a spring rod, made to look like a puppet stage. It had yellow curtains in the theater window. Each time the show was to go on, the blue curtain was hung in the laundry room doorway that gave my uncle just enough room to sit on his knees and do the show. My aunt would get a kitchen chair and set it in front of the curtain, and I waited for the show to start. I knew a few words by then and could use them in the right place, although I was prompted most of the time by my aunt. I would say, "Ta-ta-ta-da!" and the show would begin.

"Welcome to the castle of the king and queen and the royal stallion," my uncle said, just like a ringmaster at the Barnum and Bailey Circus. Then whatever came into my uncle's mind was the story for the act. It was usually full of action and sometimes a quarrel between the king and queen that always ended with them hugging and saying they were sorry. Sometimes, there would be a little part for the stallion. My uncle had the neighing sound down pat, as well as the clip-clop sound it would make as it galloped away.

When the show had to end, the king's stallion would

come out and take a bow, followed by the king and queen who would do the same. Then, in the same ringmaster's voice, Uncle Paul would say, "The End." The blue curtain and the puppets were neatly put away until the next big show.

Having autism often means a delay in communication and social skills, and they don't always come until much later in life for those of us on the spectrum. So, although I was growing older in years, my routines and behaviors did not change, and those puppet shows were carried on for many of my early years, helping me learn communication and social skills.

Aunt Lola and Uncle Paul wanted to keep me busy and safe, so they always tried to get me out for a ride to a park or somewhere safe where they could keep me corralled. A fenced-in baseball park that still allowed me to run freely without someone hovering over me was the best. I feared *nothing*. Streets, woods, water, bees, hot and cold, and even broken glass meant nothing because danger was not something I understood. So, my parents and my aunt and uncle had to be my protectors for many years. They would take me to the same places often so I could learn boundaries on what was safe and in an area that they could manage letting me have protected independence.

I remember the CDs my uncle would play on our rides. He would sing along, and when a hook was played, like "Charlie Brown, he's a clown," he would always look in the rearview mirror, positioned so I could see him while he made funny faces as he sang along. One of the CDs was of "The Twelve Days of Christmas" that made the sounds of the partridge, and he would exaggerate the beep, beep of the partridge while making funny faces in the mirror. It made me happy and taught me words and sounds. Although, at that point, I could still not use any of them constructively.

Every so often, my mom and dad would take me to the Wisconsin Dells, a tourist town a few hours away, with my brother Shaun. Everything had to be planned out, timed right, and organized to not only let me have fun but also to allow my brother to be able to have time to do what he liked. He has never really told me that I was a pain, but I am betting he would have liked to leave me at home sometimes. Most of us with autism require much time and energy, and sometimes the rest of the family has to make sacrifices. If you can find someone to care for your child with autism at times, it would allow you to take the rest of the family out for a day. I think that would let others know that they are important too.

On one of our trips to the Dells, I remember that we were leaving our room to go for lunch, and I was skipping and running my hands on the wooden railings. Almost everything in the Dells has a log-cabin look. Well, sliding my hands on the rails resulted in half of a tree under my fingernail! Not really, but it was big and not anything my mom could remove. I cried and cried, and they had no option but to get me to the local urgent care where the doctor pulled it right out. Earlier, I told you how I really did not know fear, hot or cold, or pain. I now believe that was the first time that my autistic brain registered pain. Although, it did not stop me from having fun afterward in the water.

When I went with my mom, dad, and brother on weekends, my uncle bought big window markers and would put a message in large print that we could see as we drove back home and into the small mobile home park that we all lived in. My aunt and uncle lived in the first mobile home, and it had sliding glass doors in the front that you could see from the main road as we drove in. There, in big colored letters, would be "Welcome Home, Jesse."

I started kindergarten in the fall of 2002. Public schools were *just* opening up to the idea of mainstreaming kids and not separating the kids that had no disabilities with the ones that did. I was pulled out for the more one-on-one type of learning in speech and math classes with the rest of the day spent in the regular classroom.

As I began kindergarten, I had transitioned to the school bus with an aide, Jan, the same Jan that was the driver of the van I rode into preschool. The school bus picked me up in front of my house just like the van did for preschool. The school was very accommodating, and repetition always made tasks easier, and in my beginning years, that was very important. Even though my small rural school did not see many children with autism, they really stepped up to the plate to understand and collaborate with my family and the Wisconsin Early Autism Project to do all they could to help me grow.

My kindergarten teacher, Heidi, said she remembered me very clearly and mentioned to my aunt about the day that she had a conversation with me about *The Very Hungry Caterpillar*, the book I was looking at. It was a one-sided conversation, she said, but in my gibberish, she knew I was pretty excited about the book. She also recalls making a trip to my home before the school year started so I would feel comfortable with being in her classroom. She remembered sitting on my bedroom floor playing with me, and I do have a visual picture of that time in my mind.

Each morning, when my bus passed Lola and Paul's mobile home, they were there in the front window, waving at me to let me know everything would be alright. If they had to be gone and could not be there to wave, two paper smiling faces would be taped up in the window in an attempt to assure me that they were still saying all was okay and, no matter what, they would always be there for me in whatever way they could.

As I grew older and got into the routine of school, I became more aware of things I did actually fear: vacuum cleaners, being in a room full of talking people, and loud noises to start. Then things, like going through the car wash or even going through the tunnel of Christmas lights at the big light display they'd put up each year, could set me off. I was afraid of being picked up by strangers, which made a lot of things extra difficult.

The summer I was six, my mom wanted me to take swimming lessons at our local swimming pool, and that did not turn out to be a positive experience. Swimming was something that truly scared me. I did not pass the class, but my mom didn't share that with me at that time. Even at that early stage of life, losing and not being good at something was sure to cause a meltdown for me. I did conquer the swimming, but it wasn't until around the age of eight or nine. I had no more lessons and self-taught myself by watching others. After that first successful jump off the board, I had conquered the fear that I had carried since I was six.

Also, my aunt and uncle had been taking me out about twice a month to a hotel near us that had a swimming pool, and I spent a lot of time in the pool with my uncle and got more comfortable. That helped me find my courage!

I always learned so much more visually. Getting directions from the swimming instructor never connected positively in my brain, but as soon as Uncle Paul showed me, I understood. People talking at a normal speed back then seemed to me to be like the gibberish I used in kindergarten to tell my teacher about the book *The Very Hungry Caterpillar*. My autistic brain could usually follow visually, so I wasn't completely in a lost world, but it took many years to understand written words, and again, to be truthful, some of them still remain confusing even now.

One day in fourth grade, I suddenly realized that I acted differently from the other kids. We were lined up for lunch, and I often felt anxious while waiting in line. Sometimes kids would cut in front of me, but I did not know how to speak up for myself or ask them to stop because the words would not come out. So, to calm myself, I would rock back and forth or flap my hands to help relieve that feeling I could never explain.

In the classroom, if things had kind of bottled up for me and the teacher or aide noticed, they would try and calm me by sitting with me and keeping me from all the chatter and commotion in the room to relax me. When it was time for recess, I would play by myself because at that time it was how I felt most comfortable. Sometimes, because of my behavior and being different, kids would tease me, but most of the time I did not understand that their intent was to make me feel bad. Also, there were kids that seemed to treat me differently, and I think they liked me and would sort of protect me from the bullies. Sometimes, I guess, we need to look at autism as a blessing. My autistic brain still protected me from hurtful intentions, I simply just did not understand what they were saying and that saved me many times from the tears and heartache other kids would have when faced with these situations.

When we had field trips at school, my aunt would always volunteer to be my buddy. She knew me well and was a big help as the teachers had their hands full with the kids who did not have a chaperone. These trips would tire me out, a lot, and even today, I tire easily. It isn't physical, but I just burn out mentally. So, most of the time on our way back from the field trips, I would sleep, or my aunt would have a favorite treat or toy in her bag that made the ride home easier. Plus, I would get car sick, so resting was helpful to keep me from getting sick and causing a problem.

Lola went on a few more field trips until the teachers felt I was able to handle the trips on my own with an aide to keep an eye on me.

In first grade, my class went on a field trip to a zoo, and my aunt chaperoned.

A memory from Lola:

"I was with Jesse looking at some big aquariums with fish. A colorful one caught my eye, and when I looked down again, Jesse was gone. I panicked, of course. It was the worst feeling I've ever had. I couldn't find him by scanning the room and started frantically calling his name. He still wasn't recognizing or answering his name yet, so once I found him, I had to take a moment to calm myself down, remind myself that he didn't know he was doing anything wrong, and take a breath."

This could be why still today, she has nightmares about me getting lost or losing me and not being able to find me. Autism, you see, does not only affect the person with autism but the entire family network, and not just for one field trip, but for a lifetime.

Teaching and understanding how to make a day better for

me as my life's journey continued was an ongoing process. Mom and Dad would tackle all those daily living skills like learning how to brush my teeth and take a bath. My bath times at home and at my uncle and aunts were pretty much the same. Toys, cups, and a small TV with a VCR player sat on the bathroom counter across the room from the bathtub, and only my mom and aunt changed those tapes. I was never really ready to get out of the tub until my fingers and toes looked like raisins and the water was too cold to warm up again.

They would help with schoolwork at night, which was so hard as my brain did not "see" school at home. When I got home, my brain switched off of school and was on home time. I was tired and only wanted to watch movies and have a snack. I still feel schoolwork should be done at school and not carried home to a child's few hours of home time each night. It would have saved me from anxiety and meltdowns for sure. Once supper was over, it was time to switch to getting ready for bed, as it was not a quick process and the adding of schoolwork was a nightmare for me and my parents.

On the weekends, my aunt and uncle would have "play" school time on Saturdays. It was an attempt to get me to be comfortable with the changes that were needed in my school day and how to switch my brain to each change, especially when I really did not know why I needed to. So, each Saturday, my aunt would set up two TV trays by the living room couch, one for me and one for my uncle. We had a stand-up chalkboard and a calendar for stars on the coat closet door. My aunt had actually bought books that were similar to what they used in school and were age-appropriate. The teacher was my aunt, and she would start out the day with the Pledge of Allegiance and our day began.

Whenever I was told in school or at home that I did something wrong, it would cause a meltdown, even when my aunt would tell my uncle to help with the question. So, they flipped the action so that my uncle and I would do the same lessons that my aunt had printed out for both of us. She would say, "Okay, this is your assignment," and we would both start our work. Some of the lessons were things she knew I could handle well, and when she graded it, she put a smiley face and "Great job, Jesse" on the top of the sheet. I then got to put a star or a sticker on the calendar that hung on the coat closet door, which made me very happy.

When we were about ten minutes into our Saturday school time, she would get the brass bell and ring it so my uncle and I could have recess and play. I loved that time, and sometimes we just went into the bedroom to play if the weather was bad, and sometimes we would go outside. A time was set that we could play, and she would tell us that when the big hand was on the nine, recess would be over, and we needed to come back to our desks. She rang the brass bell when recess was over, and the second half of school time began. If she saw I was struggling with an answer, she would say "Jesse, I can see Uncle Paul may be having some trouble. Can you help him?"

Not knowing her little trick, Uncle Paul would show me his problem, which just happened to be the same one I was struggling with. My uncle was able to play along while my aunt would go to the chalkboard and write it out, so together, we could put the correct answer down on both our sheets. They were teaching me in their way that it was okay to ask for help and to help others.

My family always tried to get me out to do things other kids did, but they always needed a plan for each event to avoid things that would set me off on a meltdown and not ever want to do it again. Sometimes, that meant that they would need to step in to make sure that I understood other people's actions that were normal to other kids but not to me.

There were times when my family had to convince a lifeguard to stop yelling at me, for example, because it would only scare me into doing something unsafe. Or the time when I unknowingly went into a bouncy house without paying and was being screamed at to come out. I didn't notice and just kept jumping! Everyone had to work so hard to help me transition without meltdowns or anger. The best way for me to pull myself out of a meltdown when things were racing around in my head and I was not sure what was happening was always to put me in a quiet place, watching my videos, and allow me to snuggle with my blankets. To me, those blankets were the feeling of love and the best comfort there was.

My mom would purchase some of the same blankets with the blue, pink, green, and yellow balloons on them, so if one needed to be replaced, I would accept the change. Those blankets will never be thrown away as the importance they had in my life will never leave me. They also played a major part in my special times with my mom. I do have comforting memories of the times after my mom had gone through my bath with me, put my pajamas on, and it wasn't quite time for bed. She would cuddle under the covers in her bed to relax and would ask if I wanted to get in for some cuddles. But she did not call it "cuddles," she called it "Lovins." I would crawl under the covers with her, and we would either watch her favorite television shows like *Little House on the Prairie*, *Family Feud*, or a movie she had rented. We would sometimes just talk about our day while she softly tickled my arms with the end of her fingers to relax me.

When I was eight, *Sesame Street Live* was coming to the La Crosse Center. Super Grover would be my first *Sesame Street Live* show experience. As a diversion from all the commotion inside the show, Lola and Paul bought me a stuffed Elmo; Cookie Monster; a hand toy that when you pushed the button, lights inside would spin around and around; and an Elmo helium balloon. I did pretty well for the first time at an event like that, but I think it's because I had watched so many *Sesame Street* videos that I wasn't afraid of the characters and was pretty comfortable.

According to Aunt Lola, all went well at the event and we headed back to our car after the show to go home. I was in my car seat in the back with all my new *Sesame Street* swag, wearing my red Elmo visor. It was warm in the car, so my uncle opened up the sunroof to get a little air moving. Well, it moved and also sucked my Elmo balloon right out of that sunroof and headed for the heavens. My aunt gave my uncle a look of terror, expecting a major meltdown, and quickly went into a plan of diversion.

She then made one of the worst days for me into a game, telling me to keep a close eye on the balloon so we could see where it would go. It went higher and higher until it was out of sight. My aunt then told my uncle to head to the Michaels store where she knew they sold helium balloons and bought another one to replace the one in heaven, and it seemed to satisfy me, so all was good. Another "protective freedom" outing my aunt and uncle took me to was a place called Lark Toys. It was a small wooden toy factory and toy store that had a carousel inside that I loved to ride on. The toy store was so much fun and had a small hands-on play area. This was again in an effort to get me out among other children my age.

They needed to have a plan to keep me under a watchful eye, and not just for safety, but also because I could not communicate. If an adult or child asked me a question, it would seem like I was ignoring them and could become an issue when someone wanted to have the toy I had. A bit typical of many children, but it was obvious when looking at me and how I did or should respond, people could tell there was a problem.

Most of the time, parents would direct their children away from me, which was really not at all what I needed. It was painful for my family to watch other kids and families move away from me as though I was contagious. They would, of course, use a diversion to avoid a meltdown for me, but in their hearts, they still hurt from the lack of interaction.

I recently messaged my second-grade teacher, Tracy, to let her know I was writing a book about my life with autism and wondered if she remembered anything about me when I was in her class. She told me she was very happy to hear I was writing a book and that she did have a memory of me which is somewhat ironic.

She went on to say that one day in class, we were told to write something, and I am not sure what, but I am sure I was feeling unable to pull those words from my brain and get them on paper. She said that she was walking around the room, checking on the progress the students were having and noticed I still had nothing on my paper. She leaned over and said to me, "Jesse, I am going to walk around the room again but when I get back, I want to see you writing." She did not say, "You need to start now!" but instead gave me time to process what she expected of me. Now, I am sure neither one of us remembers what I wrote or if it made any sense, but I did finally start writing.

Just like now, in collaboration with my aunt and uncle in telling my story, my aunt will say, "Okay, Jesse, it's time to write down some of the things you can remember when you were growing up." Although some of it needs a little editing, I do get my thoughts down on paper. Communication and writing will always be the pieces of autism that may improve some but will never be perfect. Even if it is one word at a time, I will share my story about growing up with autism.

CHAPTER FIVE:
My Official Normal

"The only place where your dreams become impossible is in your own thinking."
~Robert H. Schuller

Dear classmates,

I wish you knew that even though I act and think differently than all of you, I am just like you both inside and out. When I cried or had a meltdown when the day was not my day, it did not mean I was angry at all of you.

I felt like I was not loved or liked by you all when I struggled. If you see people like me alone or with tears down their cheeks, please go up to them and talk with them so they know you are there for them.

Please do not bully people because of their (dis) ability. Instead, learn about their unique (dis)ability and try to feel what its like to be in their shoes.

Outside of school is when I was able to be myself. So, the school dances were my best moments during school! Thank you so much from the bottom of my heart for being a part of those bright moments with me.

But remember, don't be afraid to talk to me and be around me, and please make sure you try to be there for others like me. Invite us to other after-school events like trick-or-treating in elementary school or school sports games in high school.

I am not mad at you because you are an important part of my life, but I am disappointed that you did not try to see the kind, sweet, loving, smart, and warmhearted boy with a great sense of humor I really am. If I had to give advice to your younger selves, I would have to say, please show up!

-Jesse

I have to admit that as I grew older, I became quite the flirt. The major problem with this is that most of the girls had no idea I was flirting with them! The summer before middle school, my mom took me into school to help me practice finding my way to classes and opening my locker. Although I couldn't quite verbalize it, what I really needed help with was how to talk to my peers and let them know I wanted to be their friend.

My uncle Paul and I have had conversations about everything from what it was like to be in his band, "Ricky Dee and the Embers," to how to give a girl a special Valentine, to his experiences in the Vietnam War. We walk, and we talk. That's just what we do. And so, over the years, we've walked and talked about what it was like to grow up and go to middle school and high school when you have autism.

When I walked in the door for my first day as a seventh-grader, because I really did not have friends that I felt I could communicate with, I would basically stand with a group who pretty much ignored me. I don't know if they ignored me because they did not know how to talk with me or because they just wrote me off as different. I pretty much just answered everything with an "oh yeah" or "right." It wasn't easy for me or them.

Most of the time, especially in seventh grade, I did not linger in the hallways but would go directly to the classroom and wait for the class to begin. I did have a teacher, Phyllis, who was designated to help me or explain a situation throughout my years at school, and I always knew I did not have to worry about something I did not understand. She would always be there for me when I needed help.

I was pretty good in school because my autism kept me focused. However, my intense need to do well was also often the cause of meltdowns. When I came home with schoolwork and I did not understand what was expected and could not explain it to my parents, our whole night was torture. As I grew older, my meltdowns changed. What used to look more like a tantrum was now so much more emotionally taxing.

I told my family that it felt like everything was spinning inside my head. All I ever wanted to know was why. Why did I have autism? Why did my life have to be so hard? Why was it so difficult for me to do my work when I knew I was smart enough? It did, and still does, hurt and feels personal to me. It's easy for me to feel like a failure and not as easy for me to remember the great things.

Sometimes, my mom would have to write a note to the teacher to explain what was going on and I would give it to my teacher before class, and they would try and explain and let me do the work in class. If there is one thing I could change in that process, especially for those on the spectrum, is to possibly change how homework is handled in school. Sending schoolwork home with us is very stressful, not only for us but also for our parents when every night they would try to help.

Since my brain didn't yet allow me to even write down the assignment in a way that made any sense, it was like a nightmare. That nightmare followed me through most of that year, and to be truthful, it carried through into the rest of my school years.

But somehow, my perseverance and grit got me on the honor and high honor roll many times in my junior high and high school years.

The next big step came in the fall of 2011. High School. I was excited to be a high school student, but was I ready or at the same level as the rest of my classmates? Like most of the kids who start high school, I felt ready, and I was focused on academics probably more so than my classmates who were not on the spectrum. Not all kids at that age are focused on academics, but more so on football, basketball, and being a cheerleader. Because of my autism, I really wasn't ready socially, and all of those extracurricular activities needed some experience in one-on-one connections that could help me into an important part of life. Things were just different for those of us on the spectrum. We could imagine friends and be social in our minds, but well, that's about as far as it would go for me.

I made it through but struggled with homework, and many, many times it caused me a lot of stress and anxiety. Putting into words what was expected of me for homework in my daily planner, which was my lifeline throughout my school years, was definitely an issue. Meltdowns were pretty common then and surely made every step to a satisfactory outcome overwhelming! I ended my freshman year with what I would call decent grades, but decent was not being perfect, and to most of us on the spectrum, we do not do well with decent and failure. Well, failure to me is pretty much the end of the world.

Although I struggled a lot more socially, I do have great memories of taking a big social step and decided to go by myself to my first homecoming dance. I had a blast dancing with my classmates, and yes, I slow danced with some of the girls. The dancing part did not take a lot of skills, but my communication skills still needed a lot of improvement. When you have autism, it takes a lot of patience and practice to carry on a conversation with other people. I knew that it would take time and practice to be able to think quickly and be able to come out with appropriate comments. That is something I still work on today.

Of course, sport stacking remained, in my opinion, my "official" normal. Later that year, I was asked to demonstrate my sport stacking at my school's talent show. There I was with kids doing piano and guitar solos, as well as dancing performances. To me, my sport stacking was as entertaining, and from the crowd's response, I think I had wowed them a bit. I was still not comfortable with speaking in front of people, so I decided to put together a routine of sport stacking to music, and when I was done, everyone stood up and cheered for me. I am sure by now you all are seeing how this sport has changed my life. I felt absolutely amazing and felt that people really loved Jesse Horn. It sure is surprising how a passion can change just about everything in someone's life.

Also, at the end of my freshman year of high school, my

second-grade teacher, Tracy, asked me if I would consider coming and demonstrating sport stacking to her class. Of course, I said yes and was excited to see her, my old classroom, and to demonstrate sport stacking to her class. The kids loved it, but Tracy also had another reason she wanted me to come to her classroom. She wanted me to meet one of her second graders, a young boy named Max.

Tracy told me that he also had autism, and she wanted to know if I would be interested in mentoring him over the summer. I told her I was, and my aunt agreed to let me do the mentoring at her house. We met with Tracy about a plan for those visits. I was able to do some scheduling around tournaments and not put too many days together as I still could get somewhat overwhelmed, and I did not want to make Max feel the same. We did bond some, and his mom and little sister would come along, so Max was comfortable too.

The main goal was just to work on typical things like eye contact and socialization, which was as good for me as it was for Max. We played outside, played games, watched television, and also included his little sister, Khloe, who was very social. I think Khloe was about three or four then and at that active age. I just couldn't believe I had somehow turned into the mentor, not the mentee.

In the summer of 2012, I had a mountain to climb. It was

something most fifteen-year-olds must face. For me, all life's steps needed to be on an adjusted time frame. I was still facing some of those early delays, so even though my age and physical appearance was that of every other kid in my class, autism still had a hold on what my brain was ready for. That next step was driving! I took the driver's ed class early that summer, which taught the rules of the road, signs, and which side of the road you should be on. Pretty important, right? Of course, all this was to prepare you for the permit test at the DMV.

My mom set up an appointment for me to take the test, and I felt ready and had studied the driver's manual. Well, I had studied, but just like other tests, none of the stuff we studied was actually on the test, so the first round was not good! Remember, failure was the end of the world for me, so there were tears. My mom and aunt were prepared as they knew me well. I was so disappointed and confused because, in my brain, I studied hard and could not understand why I did not pass. I felt defeated, and when you have autism and you don't do well at something, you feel confused, lost, and like no one understands, even your family.

Seeing how upset I was, my mom and aunt decided to take me to one of my favorite restaurants, The Pickle Factory, on Lake Pepin in Pepin, Wisconsin, to cheer me up. They explained to me that most people do not pass their permit test the first time. Let me explain how I feel. My brain is just wired differently. The circuits of sadness, confusion, and understanding seem to short-circuit at times, and they just don't reconnect as fast as it does for those without autism.

Your brain is so overwhelmed, it is like on overload and the fuses in those areas blow, and until the circuits can make the right spark to reconnect again, you can't even think.

Downtime and redirection to give those circuits the time to reconnect and start again are key for us all. It's like we don't hear even when others are trying to console us and make things better. It is very uncomfortable and sometimes when I was young it would cause unruly behavior. I was hard to handle, but as I grew, it turned into tears and a feeling of totally being alone in the world.

We rescheduled the permit test, and my aunt had made a copy of a good study guide, so we studied together, going through the questions over and over. I passed the second time, and then I could legally move on to the road piece of driver's education. First off, I want you all to know that I am sure my driver's ed teacher, Steve, kissed the ground after his first trip out in the school van with me. After that adventure, he sent a message saying that he just did not think I was ready.

I had never driven anything before and obviously was going to need a lot of practice. My aunt was so confident I could do it, so she became my driving coach. The first month, she scheduled practice nights. Thankfully we live in a small, rural area without a lot of cars. As we drove, we went through all the things that would be expected to pass the driver's test.

I wanted badly to drive to school my senior year, so that fall, Lola made an appointment at the local Division of Motor Vehicles office and I took the test. Was I perfect? No. But I was good enough to pass! I am a licensed driver. Thanks to my

Grandpa Delbert, I got my first car and drove to school almost every day of my senior year. I am very cautious, never really going past the speed limit, but I truly don't enjoy driving like most young people, and it takes a lot of encouragement to get me behind the wheel.

In the future, I hope I am able to do things independently that other people do, just in case my aunt and uncle are not there for me anymore. Driving by myself, traveling at the airport, finding love, paying bills, and many others things I need to do independently to take care of myself, and these things make me feel like everyone else. In my mind, I feel like I can do these things by myself, but at the same time, I fear that these things I need to do independently will get too overwhelming and cause the circuits in my brain to burst and cause tears if something happens unexpectedly. Even though many of these things are simple to some, they can be overwhelming to others, especially those on the spectrum. My uncle always says that is an example of having the fear of fear itself. There are moments that we need to breathe and let our brain charge up before doing that task independently so we don't get overwhelmed.

In my sophomore year of high school, I made it to another homecoming dance, reaching out for that normal everyone else enjoys. But, when I think back now, the biggest plus for me was my language arts class.

I know it doesn't sound like a place where someone with autism would find a glimpse of light at the end of a dark tunnel. However, sometimes the combination of the right assignment at the right time has the makings of a new adventure.

My teacher, Bobbi, asked that we all read a poem in front of the class after watching the movie *Dead Poets Society* starring Robin Williams, a movie I really liked. She did not assign a certain poem to any of us but put a bunch of poems in the middle of the table for all of us to pick the poem we would read for the class.

I really can't remember the poem I chose, but when it was my turn to read the poem, little did I know that it would open a door for me and was at least half of the reason I am where I am today. I practiced and practiced, and the animation I put into it caught my teacher's eye. When all the poems were read and we were waiting for the bell to ring to head off to our next class, my teacher asked me to see her before I left. She said, "Jesse, you did an amazing job reading your poem, and your eye contact and hand movements were done well."

In fact, I was the only student who used hand movements. She felt I was one of the best spoken in the class that day. For a kid with autism who struggled with communication, just maybe that was the sign of where my voice could take me. Bobbi felt that I would be good in forensics and thought that joining the club would be something I would enjoy and excel at. I told her I was interested and wanted to talk it over with my family first, and she thought that was a great idea, and if they had any questions, she was there. My family was proud of me and how well I had done with reading that poem in front of the whole class.

Remember that protective bubble my family had used for years? Well, it was time to remove it in this situation because I was comfortable, and they could see it was a place where I could be on the same level as my classmates. The interaction with my classmates outside of school was a step I was ready for. So the next day, I told Bobbi that if she still felt it was right for me, I wanted to be part of the forensics club. Now was the job of finding the right niche for me. Bobbi knew about my passion for sport stacking and that it was something I was well versed in.

In forensics, one of the areas in the competition is called a demonstration speech. We decided sport stacking would be a perfect demonstration speech for me. I spent many nights after school practicing the demonstration speech I had worked on with my family. Bobbi was so great in giving me tips on voice tone and proper hand movement. All that practice got me through the regional competition as one of the students from Cochrane-Fountain City High School going to the 2013 state competition in Madison, Wisconsin, held at the University of Wisconsin. I would travel for three hours with classmates to Madison in the school van.

At the university, there were rooms assigned to each category, and the demonstration room was quite a distance from where the others were at. My teacher was also a judge and was unable to stay with me. I was on my own and told her I would be okay doing my speech without her presence. The speech went very well, and at the end of my speech, I revealed how much the sport changed my life. How it changed someone like me; someone who lives with autism. That speech won me a silver medal at the state competition.

After my presentation, I left the room, and everything looked so big and I did not know what direction to go to get back to my teacher and other classmates. I was worried the van would leave without me (which they would never have done), but in my mind, it was a scary outcome. My mom had sent her TracFone with me, and I knew how to make a call if I had a problem or when I was back at school and needed to call my aunt and uncle to pick me up. Well, being in a big university and not having any idea how to find my group or school van, I knew I needed some help, so I called my aunt back in Buffalo City, three hours away from Madison. Luckily, she answered, and I told her what was wrong. She had tried to cover all the bases in case of a problem and had my teacher's cell number just in case she had a need to call her.

Aunt Lola told me not to hang up, to just stay on the phone with her while she used her other phone to call my teacher, who was judging another speech. Bobbi picked up and told Lola that she would send some of the others who were done to go and find me. She gave her one of their phone numbers so my aunt could guide them her best to find me. I stayed inside as my aunt told me, just in case the doors to the outside would close and lock and I would be unable to get back in. My aunt told the kids I was inside a glass foyer and they should be able to see me when they were looking where the teacher thought I would be.

She remembered hearing, "There he is," from the kids and me hanging up without saying I was okay and that they found me, but she knew that if there was any other problem, she would hear back from them or the teacher. My aunt kept calling me to make sure everything was okay and see when I thought we would be back at school so they would be there to pick me up.

I guess you could say I won a silver medal for my speech *and* for doing the right thing when I ran into a problem that day. The experience led me to join forensics again in my junior year, and I chose a poem to read, "Casey at the Bat," and surprisingly I made it to state again and won a bronze medal. Sadly, because of my class load in my senior year, I decided that all my focus and time would need to be in those classes. But what I conquered in those two years truly was life-changing for someone who lives their life on the autism spectrum.

On May 23rd, 2015, the day had finally come. Fourteen years of waiting to graduate from high school. My mom and aunt worked together on a graduation party that was held in our city community room. I was excited, but I was also sad because all of the memories of school were coming to an end. Most likely, it'd be the last day I would see the classmates I grew up with. I thought about my years in high school and wondered that if I had been able to let my classmates know about my autism sooner, I could have worked harder to be friends and help them understand and know the real Jesse.

When the principal called my name, I walked up on that stage, shook his hand, and received my diploma along with the same kids I sat with on the round rug in preschool for circle time. At that moment, I was proud of myself. After all those years of hard work, dealing with my autism, and school, it all paid off. My family and my teachers were all proud of me and hugged me and wished me the best for my future. I knew I would have never made it to that day in my life if it had not been for all of them, and I will always be grateful.

CHAPTER SIX:
Changing Course

*"I can be changed by what happened to me,
but I refuse to be reduced by it."
~Maya Angelou*

Dear Aunt Lola & Uncle Paul,

I wish you knew how much I love you both. To me, you are the best aunt and uncle in the entire world. I am extremely lucky that I have you both in my life and you have always been there whenever I needed you. I truly appreciate everything that you both do for me. My dream is to have a wife one day who loves me for who I am, spending the rest of our lives together just like you both.

I promise you I will do anything I can to continue my motivational speaking and sharing my story. Your sacrifices to get me to all of those sport stacking tournaments taught me how to use my passion and the confidence I gained from being part of our sport stacking family to start my motivational speaking career. From the bottom of my heart, I say thank you for helping me make my dreams come true. You two are such a big part of my life, and I love you both so much!

   -Jesse

Hoops, hurdles, and stress were all part of a process that seemed never-ending for my family. My dad worked, and my mom was a stay-at-home mom. My therapy had begun, and my parents and uncle and aunt went all into following the therapists' lead and used it repetitively in play, at social events, and in daily life skills. They used everything they could to reach through what seemed like a wall that I built. It took a lot of creativity to break down that wall.

In my uncle's words, "At a point in Jesse's young life, and after a year of therapy, I began to realize I would have to become his very best friend. The only way that could happen and be effective would be for me to relate to him on his level. I needed to try and think like him. This would be the start of a long and sometimes tedious adventure and commitment beyond my deepest imagination."

He goes on to recount a memory: "One day, we were walking past a small shop when Jesse noticed several small beanie baby boppers on display in the window. He asked me if he could have one and picked it up and handed it to me. I said okay, but bought all three of them for him. Little did I know how that small purchase would become such a big part of the bonding of Jesse and myself.

When we arrived home that day, he immediately started to play with these beanie boppers and wanted me to also play with them. So, I became the voices of all three of them, Rugged Rusty, Footie the soccer player, and of course, the sweet little Jazzy Jessie. Patience and imagination were a constant requirement each and every day for weeks and months. But, over those months, we began to notice how Jesse's word skills and acceptance of the outside world began to take shape.

By using all of the tools, like those mentioned, as props in real-life stories about what was going on in the outside world, I have no doubt in my mind that this set the stage for how I did reach into Jesse's mind. I am not a doctor or therapist, just Uncle Paul, but I know the progress that we were seeing was remarkable."

Another summer, my mom and dad had purchased an older Winnebago motor home with the hope that it would make times away for me more comfortable. We made several short trips locally, and my mom would take me out to just play, trying to get me used to the vehicle.

We left on a Friday to travel to Yogi Bear Park as a family. As soon as we arrived, Dad got us all settled in our camping lot, and the day progressed. It wasn't long before I decided to dart from the campsite. Of course, my dad saw me and set off in a full-on run to catch me.

Calmly walking me back was definitely not an option, he soon realized, and all he could do was pick me up and carry me kicking and screaming all the way back to the motor home where the mother of all meltdowns seemed to go on forever and ever. I know my brother and Trista had to be embarrassed and were really thinking they should have stayed home, and those camping next to us were probably not as focused on having fun while the neighbor's child was in a full-screaming meltdown mode.

Well, we made it through that day and I did sleep that

night, but my mom and dad knew that this was just not working, and if they wanted to salvage some of the vacation for the rest of the family, they would need to call my aunt and uncle who lived three hours away on that Saturday morning. My aunt said my mom was crying because she so wanted it to work for me but felt they would just have to come home.

My aunt didn't want them to not enjoy what they had saved up to do and said, "Let us get dressed, and we will come and get Jesse and bring him home with us." They drove six hours down and back to make that happen. I was always glad to go with them so it all went well, and after a quick stop at the drive-thru for french fries, we headed back, and I fell asleep in my car seat and did not wake up until we were home to my aunt and uncle's house.

I wanted to share this story because, again, the family has to be creative, patient, and very flexible. It is always a good idea to have back-up caregivers who know your child's disability and their behaviors. Being able to trust someone else with your child is always hard, but even more so when the child is nonverbal and unable to share if they have been mistreated.

Let me throw in a few tips that have worked at times with me after a bit too much stimulation or at a time where my brain did not understand a change or the words and pictures that were flying around in my head. Water! I know water is a big fear for families because a lot of children with autism are fascinated by it. However, it can also be a lifesaver. Water in the bathtub with water toys and a bubble mat that would produce a cloud of bubbles that wrapped around my whole body would almost immediately calm me down. Sometimes I could be in the tub two or more times a day depending on the level of anxiety I was feeling.

I mentioned before that videos were something else that comforted me. I had over 300 videos in my collection, with some I only watched a few times and others I watched over and over again. For the majority of kids with autism, we need extra downtime in our day. I know there are warnings about too much television or technology, but our brains have to work so hard to do school and calm our sensory needs, we often end up needing relaxation and comfort.

Knowing this, Lola and Paul were worried about me missing them while they were gone on a trip to Pennsylvania. I was very used to the routine of being with them on weekends, and they thought if they did a video of themselves doing things I loved, it would help me not miss them. This particular video showed things like my uncle counting the five rings on this game that I adored. This could possibly be useful, even with the daily trauma of dropping off your child on the spectrum with a caregiver for the day. I do have a picture my mom took of me seated in front of the television watching Uncle Paul play the counting ring game with me the week they were gone on their trip. Even now, that thought makes me smile.

Parenting is incredibly difficult, even with a child who does not have autism. But, when you add in me not understanding them and them not having a clue how to reach and redirect me, it was like a bizarre game of charades. When they figured it out and an end-of-the-world meltdown stopped, they filed that trick away for the next time. But that did not always work with my little brain, which made the circuits light up during the meltdown like the Fourth of July fireworks until they were no longer busy and could again make a connection. This is somewhat like when a phone line is busy and you are just not going to get through.

Although everyone in my family tried so hard, things definitely changed course in 2013. As most of you who have raised or are raising a child on the spectrum know, life changes, or just being unsure of how to handle life in general, is scary, and we rely on our parents to guide us through. But when your parents are having a tough time guiding their own lives, it makes things especially scary and uncomfortable.

Day after day, things seemed to get worse. My parents never fought when I was in the room, but the loud, ugly exchange of words could be heard through the walls of our mobile home. Loud plus negative talk and hurt feelings terrified me as I was unable to process what was happening and what I should do or where I should go. I always stayed in my room when that happened until my mom would come to get me up for school or for a meal.

Being in my room, pulling my blanket over my head, and cuddling with my blankets with the balloons made me feel better. Of course, those of us on the spectrum are very comfortable being alone, and that helped. It is our safety net from a sometimes scary world. My mom and dad loved me very much and were aware of how change, conflict, or confusion could bring on a meltdown for me. I know they tried hard to cover up their own struggles to try and maintain a less complicated world for me.

My mom had also been suffering from severe back pain that required surgery in hopes of getting a bit of her life back. I know now that all of this was a big strain on my parents' relationship along with money issues always haunting their lives. Most of the disagreements I heard were about money and never having enough. Well, if you can get PTSD from situations like this, I may suffer from this still today. Whenever I hear anyone who is in disagreement and if their voice goes up an octave, I immediately want to hide away until it is over. I wish I could put into words how scary this feels. Even if I'm just out shopping or at a restaurant, the sound of arguing makes me instantly sick to my stomach and I want to leave.

The only way I can explain the feeling is that it is like standing in the middle of a railroad track and a freight train is bearing down on you and you're seconds away from death. Your heart is beating fast, and your stomach has a very sick feeling. Well, I wasn't sure what would happen, but to keep my mind off all that, I followed the rules of sport stacking my aunt and uncle gave me, the three p's—patience, practice, and perseverance—to be the best I could be at sport stacking.

One day, I got home from school and my mom was in the

kitchen, crying. When I asked her what was wrong, she said, "Your dad's outside, and he wants to talk to you."

In my heart, I knew this was bad, but off I went anyway. My dad was leaning against the garage, smoking a cigarette. "Jesse," he said. "You know how hard your mom and I have been working at our problems, right?"

I nodded.

"Well, we just can't figure them out. I know this might be hard, but I'm moving out. Your mom and I are getting separated."

After a night full of tears and anxiety, Lola, Paul, and I headed to Holland, Michigan, for a tournament the next morning. This was really what I needed, to forget about what was going on at home and to get pumped up for the 2013 AAU Junior Olympic Games Sport Stacking Championships in Detroit, Michigan, that July. When the big day came to drive to Detroit for the Junior Olympics and to see all my sport stacking family, I was so excited because it is where I am most comfortable.

The hotel was in the GM building, and when I got there, I met other stackers downstairs to practice before prelims the next day and to show off a bit to spectators who were in the building. The people in Detroit were all wonderful and so polite. I was so amazed on how to get to the venue, the Cobo Center. We just walked out of the hotel and got on this little monorail system called "people movers" that circled the downtown area and had stops throughout the city, and one of those stops was the Cobo Center.

That night I reluctantly went to bed, but it was time to call it a night as prelims were first thing in the morning. As soon as I went to bed, though, all of those problems at home began to come back into my head. I really had a hard time getting to sleep. My autism held me back a lot from being able to express my thoughts and feelings back then, and I still struggle with that today. I always felt I just needed to take my mind off my feelings, and that is where sport stacking and my sport stacking family helped to get me to another place where I could forget some of those negatives in my life.

I didn't want to say anything to my aunt and uncle because I thought it would be easier for me to just put it out of my mind. Morning came, and we were up early to get to the prelims and the first day, the day that would determine if you would stack in the finals the next day. We headed out for the Cobo Center, and I felt I was going to do good, at least that was what I was telling myself, but I was wrong! I really can't explain what went wrong, but it seemed my whole day went bad. When you have autism, failure isn't an option. I struggled through my prelims like never before. I just couldn't focus, and I ended up in tenth place in my division in the 3-6-3 stack, just barely making it into the finals the next day. I was having a very hard time accepting the outcome of prelims day. That night, Uncle Paul knew something was not right and told my aunt Lola that he would talk to me about it.

As we were relaxing in our room, my uncle said, "Jesse, before we go to bed, I think we should take a walk around the hotel." We explored the hotel, but I knew he wanted to have what we call a pep talk before the big day.

"Jesse," he continued, "I am feeling something is bothering you. Do you want to talk about it?" I was so glad to be alone with my uncle and able to tell him how I was feeling about what was going on and how confused I was about my dad leaving my mom and me. I told him I felt awful, sad, and angry that he would do that, and I worried about my mom being alone. He told me that Mom would never be alone, that she had me and Shaun (my older brother), and we all have a supportive family behind us.

He said, "I know you're only sixteen, but you're going to have to be the strong one and be there for your mom."

I said, "I feel I really could never forgive my dad for what he did. I had some pretty big tears." My uncle told me that he understood how I was feeling inside and shared how his dad had walked away from his mom and seven kids when he was around eight and how he struggled with forgiveness as well. Uncle Paul dried my eyes with his hankie and said, "Life has peaks and valleys. As you get older, you will find that out and will understand all of this a bit better." He told me, "Today you are in a valley, but tomorrow you are going to the AAU Junior Olympics finals, and you are going to climb out of that valley and be the champion I know you are."

After a good night's sleep and that very important conversation, it was the big day to prove to myself that I was one of the best sport stackers in my division and in the world. It was finals day, and most of the best stackers in the United States in my age division were stacking, but I told myself to do my best and remember all that my uncle said to me. I rocked the house, with a clean sweep in my division with gold medals in the 3-3-3, 3-6-3, and the cycle. I was the 2013 AAU 15-16-year-old male overall sport stacking champion. I also received two trophies for being the fifth fastest overall male in the 3-3-3 stack in the entire tournament and fifth overall in doubles. Our team relay took third place overall.

I had proven that no matter what was going on in my life, I could push through and be the champion I needed to be.

After my dad left, though, things took a turn for the worse in my house. Suddenly, when I returned, my mom had a new boyfriend and there were new people walking around my house. I felt as though I had no freedom in my own home, which was difficult.

I was totally uncomfortable in my own home. Maybe if I had been a toddler, I could have adapted easier, but at sixteen, now there was another man invading my space. This was the life I was comfortable with and one that had stayed the same for fifteen years. There were days when I could express my feelings, but other days I was quiet and sullen.

By the end of my junior year of high school, I had attended school dances, made it to the state forensics competition, and won a bronze medal in what was a very sad time for me. Being asked to be part of the annual talent show again was also a very big help in keeping my focus on what I loved most, and that is sharing my passion. Staying focused and not letting what was happening around me got my grades from B's and C's back to the A's and B's I was used too.

I was very happy that I got back up on my feet after experiencing what I thought was the lowest time in my life. The most memorable moment of my junior year was going to my junior prom. I had attended homecoming dances, but never really thought about prom because I perceived it being so different and something I may not really fit into and wondered what others would think of me coming to prom on my own.

I thought about it a lot during my junior year, and I finally made the decision to go to prom! When I told my aunt and uncle I wanted to go, they were excited for me making the decision on my own, but not only was it short notice but was also actually the day of prom! Without missing a beat, we were off to find prom attire and then instantly off to get dressed and head out for pictures with my class. My uncle and aunt were my wheels but stayed out of the picture as much as they could so I could experience the night like the rest of my class. Let me tell you, that prom was the best time and overall school experience in general. Everyone was so accepting of me dancing with my classmates and, of course, a few slow dances with the girls.

These events were really an opportunity for me to be like everyone else and to let people see that I had a personality and sense of humor and who this Jesse they knew all their lives who had autism was really like. Good memories and a moment in time that I was whole.

During my senior year of high school, though, my home life remained unsettled. My mom's new relationship was on rocky ground. One day it was on, one day it was off. Some nights I was alone and my mom would come home in the morning to see me off to school, and some mornings she would call me from her boyfriend's house to wake me up. Now, remember, autism never just goes away, and even though I was seventeen, I felt all my security had been lost and feared not really knowing what would happen next. I wished more and more to move in with my aunt and uncle.

I tried to stay focused so my schoolwork would not suffer and spent many early evenings with my aunt working on projects for school. I talked with my uncle, and he told me that when I was eighteen, I could make my own decisions on where I lived and if I decided I wanted to move in with them, I was welcome and could stay as long as I wanted, even if that was forever. That kept me hanging in there for a while, but I knew my mom was trying hard to be there for me while also trying to start a new life.

I loved my mom more than anything, but I just could not start this new life because the combination of my autism and these difficult changes would make my life much like a bad nightmare. I kept talking with my uncle and aunt, and one weekend in the middle of my senior year, I just decided I was not going home and would live with my uncle and aunt.

My aunt talked with my mom and told her I wanted to move in with them. I was almost eighteen, and I felt I was ready to make my own decisions. Mom understood. She knew that it was a very uncomfortable place for me, and because I was so close to my aunt and uncle, she knew the move was the best thing. I know it was very hard for her to agree to the change, but she always wanted the best for me. It didn't take me long to move—most of my stuff was already at Lola and Paul's.

Little did I know that so much more would be changing very soon.

CHAPTER SEVEN:
A Horrible Joke?

*"It takes strength to make your way through grief,
to grab hold of life and let it pull you forward."
~Patti Davis*

Dear Mom,

I wish you knew how much I love you and that I love you more than you love me! You were the best mother in the whole entire world, and I am extremely lucky that I had you as my mother. You were the bravest woman in the world because you did anything to protect me and you were always there for me whenever I needed you. Even when I had the most powerful meltdowns and tears, you still loved me for being me: a boy with autism. Also, I have missed you so much every day since you decided to leave this world so soon.

Even though I am very sad that you are not physically here, I know you are with me spiritually. I know you are up there in Heaven watching me grow, learning about the world around me, and seeing the many accomplishments I have made in my life. I want you to know that I am okay and that I love and miss you so much, Mom!

-Jesse

In August of 2015, I started college at Minnesota State College Southeast. We met with the disability advisor first, who would sign me up for any possible extra support, like a quiet place to test and access to tutors as needed. I did much of my testing in a quiet room in the learning resource center, which was helpful. Also, if there was a time limit for the test, that could be adjusted for me if needed. For those of us on the spectrum, being pressured to finish a test would almost always cause anxiety and an eventual meltdown.

Many times, my anxiety would skyrocket as soon as I saw a question that hadn't been on my study materials. Even if I left that question for last, it would make my anxiety level higher, so I started second-guessing even the ones I knew. No matter how long I sat there, staring at one or two questions, the answer would not come. In the end, I just turned in the test and hoped for the best. My aunt would be waiting for me in the parking lot, and she was always patient, even when she sat for an hour or more than usual. And then would come her question: "Well, Jesse, how did it go?"

Because I was in a safe place, I knew it was okay for the tears to come. She would try and talk me down off the cliff and always said that I could send a message to my advisor, Cindy, about the issue, and she would let me know it would be okay and how even if I had two wrong, it really would not affect my grade. I always asked for additional projects that I could do that would lift my grade. Some teachers were good with that, and some were not. My passion for sport stacking was a blessing. It was my friend, my coach, and what helped me pull back out of my head from the constant chatter that would say to me that I was going to fail that test. All my brain circuits would find their right connections and positive electricity would be back up and running.

My advisor, Cindy, was always there for me, letting me know that she would guide me to be as successful as I could be. Even though she had to follow all the rules with me as she did with all her students, if I asked for help, she was there. We became dear friends, and I will always have a special place in my heart for her. When I entered college that year, I took the individualized studies program that was math-heavy. The program was one you could receive an associate's degree in, and at that point, after discussing my future with my aunt and uncle, we thought something in the accounting field may be the best career choice for me.

Then, with the degree and my grades and the school behind me, it could be possible to work with a company as an apprentice and see where it would take me. I had decided to do the associate's program in three years rather than the two to try and not overload myself, knowing that college was much different than high school and there would be even more time needed for each class.

For those of us on the spectrum, idioms and slang can be similar to trying to understand French when you don't speak it. I am a bit better at that now, but I'm still learning. For example, this story is a little off-color, but true. Recently, I did a presentation to Hurley Elementary and Junior High School, and the night before, we stayed over the border in Ironwood, Michigan. We decided to go to a restaurant in Hurley for supper called the Iron Nugget. They had many area historical articles on the walls. Oh, by the way, the food is amazing!

Anyway, next to our booth, there was an article on the wall about the killing of a woman who was a beautiful and popular lady of the night in town. I read the article out loud to my aunt and uncle. All the while, they knew that to me, the lady of the night probably just meant she liked the nighttime. Typically, for some of us on the spectrum, until we experience the terms, we don't really know the true meanings. When I was done reading, my aunt said, "Jesse, do you know what a lady of the night is?" Of course, I said, "Not really," and she told me, and I said, "Oh, okay then." Funny, but true.

So, when you are working and talking with someone you know has autism, remember, slang and idioms don't always help explain the situation or the job you want them to do. We are literal thinkers. I hope that helps others maybe understand that really we are not slow. Our brains just function differently, and we really are intelligent people you really want to know and work with. It didn't take me long to feel comfortable with my surroundings at school, although lunchtime still mirrored high school. Most of the time, I ate alone, except for a few times when Dylan, a student, and friend from my high school, had classes at the same time I did, and that was great!

Life after high school was falling into place. I had a good relationship with my teachers, and my schedule worked so well for me.

That is, until October 3rd, 2015, around 8:30 p.m., when my world changed forever. I was just two months into my first semester of college, and the night had started out as a normal night for me: checking my social media for messages or posts from my sport stacking friends.

My uncle came into my room and told me he would be right back, and I knew my aunt had left the house earlier. At first, I wondered where they had to go. I continued looking at my messages when, all of a sudden, I knew something was happening. An ambulance and other vehicles, including the police, had come through the road in front of the little mobile home park we live in. I walked out on the sidewalk and could see that they were all parked in front of my mom's mobile home.

I had no idea what was going on. I had just talked with my mom on Facebook Messenger a few days earlier, and she was telling me how excited she was about the news that my brother and his wife were expecting their second child. She told me how she wanted a girl, but also said she didn't care as long as the baby was born healthy.

I was very concerned as I watched all the lights at her house, and at first, my mind thought that my mom may be having major back problems again, as even after all her surgeries she had so much pain and I thought it may have gotten worse. As I stood outside, I really did not know what to do. Thankfully, my neighbor, Ashley, stopped me from walking up to my mom's house and just gave me a warm hug while we watched the ambulance. Then, I caught sight of my uncle walking slowly back toward me with a stunned look on his face and making no eye contact with me. He said, "Jesse, we need to go in and have a talk." When we got into the house, I asked him if everything was alright with my mom. What happened to her?

My uncle looked at me and said, "Jesse, your mom is gone. She passed away." I was immediately in shock and thought this all must be a horrible joke my uncle was sharing with me. I couldn't believe him.

But my uncle just said, "I am so sorry, Jesse. I am telling you the truth." Tears poured out of my eyes and ran down my cheeks. I hugged my uncle tight, knowing the reality of this moment in my life and my family's lives. My aunt came into the house and hugged me, and we all cried. She was looking for some paper that had my mom's handwriting on it. She didn't explain why, but I would learn later on what had really happened to my mom.

My head hurt so bad from crying and thinking about all the moments and great memories I had with my mom and knowing she was no longer with me. Other family members started to come to the house and gave me hugs and told me how sorry they were for my loss. That night was the worst night of my life and the first night in my life I was sleepless the whole night. That morning, the pastor of our church came to give us his condolences and offered anything he could to help.

As of today, it is four years since my mother took her life. Although there were so many things I couldn't understand, and so much pain to endure, in a way I believe my autism may have been a blessing. My brain is literal, and although you go through the same emotions, something lets us see it in a different light and we are able to go on.

I did not go to the graveside service for my mom. I felt I had come to terms with the loss, and I wanted to carry on that day as normally as I could. My uncle stayed home with me while my aunt went, and when she came back, we went to Eau Claire and spent the day together mending our hearts in the way I felt was best.

My uncle told me that when I was ready, he would take me to the cemetery to say my goodbyes. He took me to my mom's grave a few days later where he left me to talk to Mom but kept a watchful eye on me in case I needed his support. That day, I told mom that I would miss her and I loved her, and even though I experienced this tragedy, I would not let it stop me from moving forward in school and doing what I love in life. I promised her that I would make her proud, that even though this horrible thing had happened to us, I had to have hope.

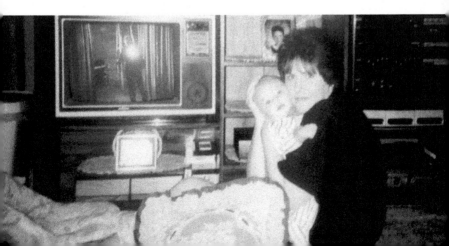

CHAPTER EIGHT:
I Am Autism

"If I could snap my fingers and become nonautistic,
I would not. Autism is part of what I am."
~Dr. Temple Grandin

Dear Younger Self,

I wish you knew that your autism will allow you to be a blessing to others. I wish I could tell you that even though things are hard now, they will get better.

I wish you knew that your loving heart will be a key to others gaining a better understanding of autism. That you should trust your heart to follow the footsteps laid out for you.

Please never forget that your autism does not define you. You define autism.

You are exactly who God meant you to be, and the gift of autism supplies the light behind your star.

Don't ever give up.

-Jesse

"My name is Jesse Horn, and I have autism. I'm also a world champion sport stacker, a motivational speaker, and I was a guest star on the TV show *The Doctors*."

On October 25th, 2017, I gave my very first professional speech. I stood up in a room full of teachers and therapists and the state Department of Public Instruction employees and told them about my life. I shared with them how difficult it is to navigate through life, but that it isn't necessarily because I have autism. It's because life is difficult.

I told them how watching one commercial on TV had opened up doors for me, which then opened another, and then another, just like it would for anyone. Well, for anyone who is ready and willing to do the speech.

Although I was nervous, I had practiced my speech over and over and felt very confident in what I would share. I could tell that I was connecting with the audience, as their attention, head nodding, and overall reaction made it clear that I had made a positive impact that day.

When I said my last line, the people in the room stood up. I'm positive you couldn't have wiped the smile off my face at the sight of my first ever standing ovation.

I was beaming with pride. After many uncertain years, Jesse Horn had a purpose. As soon as we got back into the car that day, I turned to Lola and said, "Aunt Lola? This is going to be my job. I am going to be a motivational speaker."

Recently, I was named a Rising Star by the River Valley Media Group. In December, I am contracted to do a speech in El Paso, Texas, and that will be my 20th speech. And I sure won't be stopping there. I'll be rising, just like the award says.

You might be thinking that my story is sad—autism, my dad leaving, my mom dying by suicide—but that's not why I'm here. I'm here because I will never NOT have autism.

Some of us will never be totally worldly. We may still flap our arms when we get excited, may carry on a conversation with ourselves, and others of us may never be comfortable driving a car.

Many of us will never totally understand safe and unsafe, or some may take advantage of us in different ways because we lack the ability to read people's true intentions. We can be very set in our ways, and if we think we are right, even though we are so off the path, it can push people away if they truly don't understand that it is autism and not just us wanting to be confrontational.

I know it is very hard to learn to love and be a part of our lives sometimes, but hey, in my life I think I have seen this often in those who call themselves normal. I do know that with one in fifty-nine kids being diagnosed and no really true answer to why and where this difference in our brain comes from, it is going to take a lot of patience and understanding because all of us with autism are going to play a major part in the decades to come.

I also know how EASY it is to love and be a part of our

lives sometimes. I have a huge heart, I am fun to be around, and I'm kind and honest. There are certain ways that my brain functions that have helped me to become a world champion sport stacker.

Recently, I realized that my dreams of helping people can have a much farther reach than I ever imagined. I was online one night, checking my social media outlets when I noticed a message that was entirely in Spanish. Looking closer, I realized that I could use translation to read the message. It was from a woman named Dayana, who lives in Venezuela. She has a little boy named Daniel, who also has autism. She was reaching out to me to thank me for giving her hope.

Hope that Daniel would be successful someday.

Hope that Daniel would be kind and polite like I am.

Hope that Daniel will find a passion.

Hope that Daniel will find friends and be loved.

Hope that somehow she could get Daniel the help that he so needs, even living in a country where that is MUCH more difficult to obtain.

Since then, I've been messaging with both Dayana and Daniel from time to time, and they've become like family to me. We send pictures back and forth, and I am so honored to keep up with Daniel's life and how he is growing and learning. It is an honor. And that hope is what propels me forward and helps me know I won't ever give up.

I have always wanted to make a difference, even if it's for just one child on the spectrum. If I can help do that, I will know that my time here on earth was for a purpose. Every person needs a purpose, and sharing my story of growing up with autism and making a difference in people's lives is mine. In order for everyone to find their purpose and life passion, we all must be included and accepted in every aspect of the world. All of us want to be loved and truly have much love to give back. We will also need a bit of space at times to get the circuits in our brain to reconnect and get back on track.

Autism isn't something that goes away. It's not something that I necessarily want to go away.

My autism is part of me, but it does not define me. I define autism. There were times when life was stacked against me, but against all odds, I came through stronger than ever, and I am proud to be who I am.

I am Jesse.

I am a speed stacker.

I am a motivational speaker.

I am a son. I am a nephew. I am a friend to many.

I am an author.

I am autism.

This gives me amazing hope for some of the students I work with. I would love for their parents to be able to hear Jesse speak. I really needed this inspiration today!

Dear Jesse,

Thank you so much for comming to Sand Lake and showing us the AMAZING speed stacking. I was amazed with how fast you are at stacking cups.

Thank you

You are such an insperation my son is going to be 6 yrs old next month and he has autism. It has been a long road so far and hearing your speech you lifted my spirits an I know my son will also have a great future.

4-8-19

Dear Jesse Horn,

Thank you for the awesome show! I was amazed! You are one of the coolest people in the world! I tried to do it! How can you do it with autism.

Thanks,
Addilyn
Room 135

ACKNOWLEDGEMENTS

Wow, this is hard because there are so many people who ave supported me and helped bring me to this point in my life. I wish I could list you all, but the list would be longer than my book. I want you to know that from the bottom of my heart, I thank you and love you all!

My book would not even have been written if it wasn't for Lillian (Lily) Rider, Itinerant Services Director for the Cooperative Education Services Cooperative (CESA 4) in Wisconsin. Lillian not only encouraged me but challenged me to make it happen. We took her challenge, and here I am saying thank you, Lily, for supporting and believing in me.

My aunt and uncle have both been my rock in everything I do, and I appreciate all they have done for me.

Now, to find someone like Christy Wopat, author of *Almost a Mother: Love, Loss, and Finding Your People When Your Baby Dies*, to see the worth of my story, pitch it to Shannon Ishizaki, owner of TEN16 Press, and become my writing coach was a blessing indeed. And thank you, Shannon, for helping me get my book on the shelves.

Last, but not least, Bob and Jill Fox, founders of Speed Stacks® and the World Sport Stacking Association, thank you for being part of my book and writing the beautiful foreword. To the World Sport Stacking Association and Speed Stacks® for believing in me and supporting me. The sport gave me the passion I needed to break through the bubble of autism. I am blessed and grateful!

Jesse L. Horn continues to excel in the world of Sport Stacking, while also using his voice to inspire those with autism. His goal is to let every person with autism know that they are much more than a diagnosis. They are capable and worthy of finding their passions and running with them as far as they can. With patience, perseverance, and a curious mind *everyone* can find a passion that brings them joy and fulfillment in their lives.

If interested in booking Jesse for a presentation, please visit jesselhorn.com for more information.

CPSIA information can be obtained
at www.ICGtesting.com
Printed in the USA
BVHW040545171121
621781BV00012B/809